Don Spen

Sing Your
Times Tables

Published 1999
Redwood Audio
a division of
Hinkler Book Distributors Pty. Ltd.
17-23 Redwood Drive
Dingley, Victoria, 3172, Australia

Illustrations by Danny Kneebone

ABC for Kids logo licensed by the Australian Broadcasting Corporation, 1999.

ISBN 1 86515 055X

Designed, printed and bound in Australia

2

1	x	2	=	2
2	x	2	=	4
3	x	2	=	6
4	x	2	=	8
5	x	2	=	10
6	x	2	=	12
7	x	2	=	14
8	x	2	=	16
9	x	2	=	18
10	x	2	=	20
11	x	2	=	22
12	x	2	=	24

3

1	x	3	=	3
2	x	3	=	6
3	x	3	=	9
4	x	3	=	12
5	x	3	=	15
6	x	3	=	18
7	x	3	=	21
8	x	3	=	24
9	x	3	=	27
10	x	3	=	30
11	x	3	=	33
12	x	3	=	36

6

1	x	6	=	6
2	x	6	=	12
3	x	6	=	18
4	x	6	=	24
5	x	6	=	30
6	x	6	=	36
7	x	6	=	42
8	x	6	=	48
9	x	6	=	54
10	x	6	=	60
11	x	6	=	66
12	x	6	=	72

7

1	x	7	=	7
2	x	7	=	14
3	x	7	=	21
4	x	7	=	28
5	x	7	=	35
6	x	7	=	42
7	x	7	=	49
8	x	7	=	56
9	x	7	=	63
10	x	7	=	70
11	x	7	=	77
12	x	7	=	84

8

1	x	8	=	8
2	x	8	=	16
3	x	8	=	24
4	x	8	=	32
5	x	8	=	40
6	x	8	=	48
7	x	8	=	56
8	x	8	=	64
9	x	8	=	72
10	x	8	=	80
11	x	8	=	88
12	x	8	=	96

9

1	x	9	=	9
2	x	9	=	18
3	x	9	=	27
4	x	9	=	36
5	x	9	=	45
6	x	9	=	54
7	x	9	=	63
8	x	9	=	72
9	x	9	=	81
10	x	9	=	90
11	x	9	=	99
12	x	9	=	108

10

1	x	10	=	10
2	x	10	=	20
3	x	10	=	30
4	x	10	=	40
5	x	10	=	50
6	x	10	=	60
7	x	10	=	70
8	x	10	=	80
9	x	10	=	90
10	x	10	=	100
11	x	10	=	110
12	x	10	=	120

1	x	11	=	11
2	x	11	=	22
3	x	11	=	33
4	x	11	=	44
5	x	11	=	55
6	x	11	=	66
7	x	11	=	77
8	x	11	=	88
9	x	11	=	99
10	x	11	=	110
11	x	11	=	121
12	x	11	=	132

1	x	12	=	12
2	x	12	=	24
3	x	12	=	36
4	x	12	=	48
5	x	12	=	60
6	x	12	=	72
7	x	12	=	84
8	x	12	=	96
9	x	12	=	108
10	x	12	=	120
11	x	12	=	132
12	x	12	=	144